CROW FUNERAL

poems by Kate Hanson Foster

Crow Funeral
Kate Hanson Foster

POETRY

ISBN 978-1-934894-78-1

BOOK DESIGN: EK LARKEN

COVER DESIGN: BERT FOSTER

COVER ART: DICK FOSTER, *THE POEM*

CONTENT EDITOR: MATT W. MILLER

EastOver Press encourages the use of our publications in educational settings.
For questions about educational discounts, contact us online:
www.EastOverPress.com or info@EastOverPress.com.

PUBLISHED BY

EASTOVER
— PRESS —
ROCHESTER, MASSACHUSETTS
www.EastOverPress.com

CROW FUNERAL

CONTENTS

III

IV

Total omniscience is a lot to expect,
even from a crow.

—from *Bird Brains* by Candace Savage

Mother is the name for God
in the lips and hearts of little children.

—William Makepeace Thackeray

One for sorrow,
Two for joy,
Three for a girl,
Four for a boy,
Five for silver,
Six for gold,
Seven for a secret,
Never to be told.

—ORAL TRADITION MAGPIE RHYME

Crow Funeral

No one notices the dead crow
alongside the road, soft underbelly exposed,
neck broken from the fall.   No one hears

the harpocratic ghost among leaves, the muteness
of all is said and done—the last
invisible breath in an air sac breaking out, breaking away.

We hear the murder, the hysterical,   full
to bursting cries.   Hundreds of wings collecting
in ceremony like a starless lake no one can enter.

No one sees the plane vanish over the ocean,
no one feels the thick multitude of salt and sky
take hold, metal cutting or not cutting the water.

And how the earth goes on breathing, stubborn
in its own perpetuity.   We let our voices explode
between us. The TV glows and hums, an ongoing

procession of make meaning, make me
understand.   Why can't we put our finger on this
and drag it back, like an oil slick across a computer screen?

The crows scold loudly as if to say look:
look at one of us fallen,   see the danger,
feel how it hurts—the dead crow sizzling

on the pavement like a fallen roof shingle.   So nothing,
so gone this thing we have lost.
No one finds the plane.   Instead we count

the days since the vanishing. A digital clock
spins numbers like a tiny planet on the corner
of the TV.   Headlines roll and ask questions:

Is this God?   Is this terror?
Someone needs to find the plane, find the answer.
The crows disperse slowly, silently.   A few at a time,

and then more.   They know sooner or later
to move on.   The clouds always let go,
the wind falls apart.   Everyone knows sooner or later

we have to stop counting.   There will be something
new to cry out for. Something else to gather
and dress us all in black.   And there will be urns and roses,

a chorus of music—a poem or prayer
will get it just right.   God or no God,
let us make it more   than what it is.

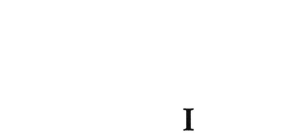

I

A Proposal

Call me your girl—your darling
dear X, uncreated. Wed and bed me
in open ocean unknown. Offer over
your errors, strip me the purpose
of wings and the brightness of blossom.
Cover my flesh in chaos, in fevers,
and fingers. For worse, for worse, scratch
a match on my walls, and burn my name
in flame—set my devils to wind, release
my signature in a strangle of smoke.
Let your aches throb through me
and mold my metals blank in our every
ember. Split me and stitch me again
and again, however you can, however
many times it takes, just make me a mother.

Nesting

The goal is to twist away

the light—a platform
of strong sticks and dry twigs,

a few strips of bark should make it hold.

And the rest is muck,
some grass and moss, a bed

for my undressing

brood patch, swollen
and warm with blood.

These secrets I keep

under me, sheltered from wind
and storm, I turn them right-side

up when they begin to pip.

No one told me how—said shed
a space on your body,

the waiting is yours only. No one

said the mouths would be nameless,
but I fed them anyway. I took

the debris they left behind and swallowed it.

Swaddle

I firmly press his body
inside the cloth—first one

point of the diamond—then another,
then another. Just enough

room for breath and nothing
else. How quiet he becomes—

a little bud before the push,
a bird egg back inside

the nest, head peeping
out. Eyes that say this is all

just the beginning.
It is crucial that we get it right.

Five for Silver

Five crows restless

in the backyard pines. The blade

that scored the bread dough gleams

from both edges. Flour clouds

the mixing bowl in the stainless-steel sink.

I think I smell the past—my grandmother's

spoons. Campfire ash. Sun puddles

flaring in the pavement. I feel

the soft choking from the ordinary

chain around my neck. My husband

is getting ready for work, his razor

tinging alarm into the porcelain. The baby

curls inside my arms—a thin film

of sweat between us. So hot and cold

the pinpricks of those shiny black pupils.

Five crows restless in the backyard pines.

The red-tailed hawk now rising.

Knead

You know this sound
by heart: the short
jingling confidence
of your car keys hurried
back onto the hook.
And the humiliated
shadow that enters you
again. This house
that shelters you—
sometimes it carries
you away in a net.
Sometimes you put
your hand on the faucet
just to watch cold water
rush down the sink. Go
ahead and latch the broken
screen door outraged
by wind. Pull dead
vegetables from the fridge.
Measure the day in dinner
bells; how many times
the dog shits in the yard.
Hold yourself up
like yesterday's daffodil—
a bloom before the spoil
and wither. Press
your fingertip into
the chip of the fruit
bowl. You were a new
melody once. The crackle
of a fresh-lit wick.
Fold the oil of your hands
into the bread dough—

the world is thick
with worn-out words—
you must knead as if
longing had a taste.

Three for a Girl

I call you Maeve
for the way it purrs peacefully
through my bottom lip and teeth.

Big-bellied god of your twirling,
I make your name a sound to save you
from the anomalies on your sonogram.

Three cysts in your brain.
The doctor points to the darkness in the photo,
fluid looming like thunderheads between cells.

There is nothing we can do
but wait, he says. Wait—a tongue
and mouth slap word.

Pregnancy is wait. Test results
are wait. I wait through trimesters
like an anvil cloud eating the updraft.

There is no need to worry, the doctor says.
Cysts often resolve themselves as the baby
grows. Outside the window, three crows

descend upon the guts of a thing
I cannot see. *Three for a girl*, my third
child, *Maeve*, my only prayer.

Housebroken

You hurl yourself around
the corner like a barn swallow whirring
your one firm mantra: *mama,*
mama, mama, mama.

I am already tired.
The morning already long.
And as your lilliputian legs scud through the house,
noises sprout loudly—a toy bin tumbles,
and wooden letters hit the floor,

a clap
for each sound
I have yet to teach you.

There is something you don't see
pressed between the wall
and the wood grain—a scrap
of old finger food that you will find,
and I will take away.

I am cautious—the mother wolf
spider tucking the black lamp cord
back under the couch.
Everything you have is bright—
like the spectacular paint
stains on your fingers.

I begin the magpie rhyme
on command—*One for sorrow, two for joy*—
The dry sound of a housefly teases
the countertop.

Three for a girl—
I only want to please you.

Seconds pulse
slowly from the clock 4, 5, 6. *Seven*
for a secret—even if I wanted,
I could not catch the fly. *Never to be told.*
I let the animal inside me lie down.

Now I Lay Them Down to Sleep

The children are not baptized.

Their souls coil
into the bed sheets, unclean,
untouched by invocations.

I am their Creator.

The exaggerated ill-illuminate.
No numina, all-seeing silence—

God is the stinkbug
on the window screen
clinging with its sour weight.

A secret fish-breathing
inside death, black
over black,

so be it.

The Sentinel

Crisis clings to the shelf
of my wings.   In my many mirrors,
I parse danger from dangerous.
I fear the unknown in the understory
to let you loose in an open field.
I know something of starvation—the discipline
of suspicion and its endless hunger
of hollows. You might say I have lived
too much, the worry has done me in.
Don't you see?   What *could be*
is the monster. Buried in needles
of twilight—this dread, a moth pulse inside me.

II

The First Gunshot

The first gunshot is not a gun—
it is a child playing with bubble wrap,
and small innocuous feet need the weight
of a whole body for a single, satisfying pop.
The first gunshot is a smile. A laugh. A fool
lit a firecracker in the hallway and someone
is going to ring a neck. There is no puzzle
in the echo—it is the muffled bone-snap
of a branch outside. The backfire of an old truck
turning the corner. The first gunshot is one
last pure breath, and the peace in the peak
of it. An unexpected flower in full vivacious
bloom. Not the start of something. A finger.
A trigger. A round. Not the first cave hollowing
within a body. Not a body hitting the floor
thinking how can I look dead enough—eyes
open or shut. Not run like a deer to the nearest
exit. Not resolving one's body as a shield to cover
a lover, a friend, a child. The first gunshot
is a cloister of joy. A sweet stillness, so alive,
so simple, after a burst of a big bright balloon.
No fear. No fight. No flight into action because
it's not going to happen. Not to you. Not today.

On the News

Another body has been buried,

and yet, there is still no page in the prayer

book ready. No wick in the candle long enough.

There is no song for that same old story—*metal*

entered the body like the first heavy raindrops landing

circles into a pond. No—the body is folded quietly

back into earth. The body behind a thin skin

of glass now, catching its first hair of dust.

Another mother hooks a body onto a nail

in the wall. There is nothing left

to do now but grow like shot

weed around it.

Joan

Joan is waiting for Jesus.
All day she weaves verse into her sun-
spoiled waiting. Babylon is falling.

Do not love the world or anything in the world.

Deep State is the shadow,
but the substance belongs to Christ.
A bowl of wrath has spilled storm and sickness
upon the earth. Socialism is dispensing
God's riches. But Joan's name is written
into the Lamb's book of life. It is as true
as lint circling the folds of her tired couch,
the bore of her gun that cannot be stolen.

Joan knows all of my sins
and judges them quietly. Nothing
of earth surprises her. I will die
with the sound he made in my bed, I tell her.
My heart still sticks to the heat of it.
It does not matter what I have done.
The tongue is a fire. All of my errors,
my common cravings, are few
among many natural disasters.

If anyone loves the world, love for the Father
is not in them.

There is so much Joan needs
to forgive. It is a chore, just like anything else—
feathers she must pluck off a wicked bird.

You cannot argue someone out of who they are, she says.
In my world, you simply take a feeling and begin
inside of it. Eventually, you will see
how right it becomes. Truth
limned in the fewest strokes.
Hail falling from heaven is just salt
in the soup.

Seek Him and ask Him to save you, Joan says.

*If you love the world, it will pass away
and take you with it.*

Elena Says

Elena has news. Elena has amazing,
great, big news.

Not all of life is tragedy.　　　I want
you to know me,

Elena says.　　　My drunk heart
in the old countries.

I want your hot barehanded grip
on my neck, your mouth

to my ear, and the words of the book
we cannot write.

Elena says she is a good girl.
A church girl.

A save-the-world girl.　　　The men
say *Elena, Elena,*

Elena, you are still beautiful. The nets
of their hands

waiting to catch her spectacular,
fevered, fainting.

It is not her fault Elena can't take that body off.

I am trying to help us be friends,
she says, but how

can you just gaze above fire
like there is no fire?

Your silence is the lull between bell
tolls, asleep

in its own tepid water.
You've never even heard

me sing!   This sun in my throat
and how it rises,

and all the dark things that exit.
Tell me now,

your favorite song.   Show me
your monster, the interior

you.   Can't you see?
The tips of the waves are frothing,

and you are
always a deep sea

away. I just keep having big news
to share. Just now

a bird has landed on the bare wrist
of a branch. It is so wonderful, Elena

says, how it springs gently inside
of its own weight.

It is all I can do to make you see it.

A Bag of Dirt

Franz—you were right. The machine churned
out too many masters; we awarded the sky more moons.

Victims toll like church bells. The saviors file in,
nowhere and everywhere. We must speak.

I think I might be my greatest disaster. Master of my address,
fingers clicking affirmations into the street wires.

Outside, old snow refuses to melt. Dirty white piles cling
to their positions. It is so ugly here, so horrifically safe.

Words scroll by like ash flicked out of a car window.
Language roils black starlings inside a white screen sky.

Dear Maggie, I do not need a blizzard of platitudes, I only want
to be still inside my own deficiency—to find the better words.

So white the sin in my skin, so blue the flames in my wrist.
I believe I have checked myself into my own vanishing.

Oh, Kaveh. Oh, Ilya—if the letters of your beautiful
names could lick me clean; if I could find the sentence to please you.

This bag of American dirt—for all its granular multitudes,
I love how useless it is, like the character count inside of a tweet.

We Who Are Nothingness

Gulp ugly
everything—
face the faceless
road kill. We suck
the wireworms—pluck
tongues of slaughter-
house waste. Love
cannot fill us; no
dream-caress
nor actual. Turn
the cow pies in
the pasture to snag
the dung beetles—
attack the fawn
at all angles. Come
infinite answer
to our infinite
want—because
there is nothing
desire cannot split
open. Nothing
need can't catch
before it lands.

She Was

She was mother. She was
body in house, dedicated

to bleach until shine
spilled across porcelain.

She was feminist—flame
struggling to break from candle.

She swallowed a pill
that removed herself from her-self.

She joined ordinary people
in the bottom-up insurgency.

She plucked delicate excesses;
untied God from her body

and let her skin spill
in the purple penitential light.

She was problematic
to the coddled American mind.

She had the eye of a woman looking
to leap from her own painting.

She was not old or wise,
and no longer pretty.

She was a waterless
blessing. An empty garden.

And when she fucked
she was man and woman,

crashing her selves on herself,
glad to be crushed by her own redundancy.

She was suffering—
cinder flashing heat back into fire.

Seven for a Secret

I check all the right boxes
on the questionnaire—
I do not want to hurt
myself or others. I am not
scared. I do not cry
all the time—panic for no good
reason. I am sleeping.
I look forward to the enjoyment
of things. I hand the clipboard
through the glass window
and smile, and a reflection
slides back, faintly female,
rat hair rising with the upwind.
I would never blame myself.

The Birds

The birds fly out. The birds fly out.
A simple unthinking, possessed

by metaphysics—an urge
or inkling to move on.

The sound of their leaving
splits me. I lie in bed,

an insufficient woman,
limbs sporadically gone

numb as if bound
by some tenuous intervention.

I have no way of knowing how
or why I will be discarded.

First a hand, then an arm—
when it needles my head I panic

and shake it all back. My eyes
reach for the window. The birds fly out.

I wanted the children. The clatter-
packed house, the perfect messes—

hot fevers I could make
better, hot fever of my husband's love.

Sometimes one kiss from a wet mouth
makes me new again,

for a while. The birds fly out.
A cold ache. Outside my husband

and son are stacking firewood.
Breathing in the dirty scent

of cut oak, maple, birch—brown
on brown on brown.

There is an art to this,
the stacking—place the cut

ends into the scent of danger—
the most prevailing wind.

My husband's instructions,
my five-year-old—his little hands,

little pink face. I pack this memory
neat into my mind.

I don't know when I became
so afraid. I don't know why

so often. I lie in bed,
watch the window, and wait.

Later I will go downstairs
and push iron into fire,

flame chewing on wood until
it takes it all completely.

Yes—later I will feel better.
For now, the birds fly out,

going south, going somewhere.
What is the name of that tree—

half dead and dripping
with squirrels? Tell me

again the name. The birds
fly out. I should mention

the wind but I forgot how it feels
when it feels good.

In one formidable blow,
the birds fly out.

I am anxious. I am moldered.
I should mention the sky.

Wean

You should know it hurts,
I think to myself. Her new body wired
for this. My third child, like the others,
a good latch from the start.

It has always been easy for me
to offer myself in this way.

Days measured in ounces, minutes,
and then hours latched to each side.
One cry, and I freeze—milk lets down,
and my shirt saturates, my body always so ready.

But I know the hard part fades. The pain stops.
The milk supply levels out. And I begin to crave
our time alone, my single starling—
the primitive pause, life nursing life.

You should know it's all going to end, I wish
someone would have told me.
That soon I would become unwired.
I would have to give away my milk
for brown bottles on the nightstand.
Limp and weak with pills, arms
fumbling to stop her rooting, my husband
downstairs warming the formula.

You should know how much it hurt
to let her fly away like that.

Vessel

Mothering, like surrender,

is something you do very well—

like the way oar tongue and water

understand each other. You've locked

your wrists to young bodies, the weight

of to-do lists. Hasty needs finger you

like branches brushing against a bird.

Downstairs there is a hurt only you can fix

belly-weeping its way up—a fist knocking

on the watching wall you hide behind.

Move aside the stock threads of that empty dress—

the strands of streets you will never travel.

Go, you say.   *Go back into the water.*

Cockcrow

How soft the early light—like an inner thigh.

And then a patchwork of white warnings—sucking

the night out shade by shade. This is the moment

my body rejects itself. I reach for my mouth

and feel the everything of emptiness.   Light

that tugs on my nerves.   Light that sears and singes

my worth.   I was a wife.   Light that makes the fog

foggier.   I was a mother.   Outside the pines

are swaying in the morning sun—new ends

growing and reaching to please it.   I had a mind.

I had ideas.   And a beast seeps through unweaving

me thread by thread,   turning its bundle

of claws—   I was I was I was.

911

There is no room for God

on the gurney, as I am placed

into the back of the ambulance.

No God in common madness—

a waste of time and resources,

as the driver calmly radios

"anxiety" and slowly rolls

me away. No God in the salt

of my night sweats or the current

of cancers snaking through

the wall. The fear of my children

dead in their beds, collapsing

into terrible, inevitable endings.

No God when I want to jump

from the bedroom window to feel

a pain I can identify—a break

that might scoop me away

from my emergency—who

wouldn't scream 911? God doesn't

know a thing about mothers.

III

Elegy of Color

Green shutters—white house.

Paper whites in the weak western light.

Brown mouse and its brown hush

across the stairs, four daughters

brushing long brown hair. Brown

beer in Black Label cans, black bible

on the nightstand. Baby Jesus

on the wall—incarnadine cheeks.

Shimmering red rosary beads. Red

garnet of my Claddagh ring. A leak

yellowing in the ceiling. The many

colors of my father singing. I was blessed

and I was blessed, like foreheads, like palm

wisps, like water my mother bought

from the church—colorless, colorless.

Birds of a Feather

My mother always told me I was a miracle.
Her pregnancy a long, slow accident

just waiting to happen. I was a drip
she feared falling down her pant leg.

My mother prays to a chain of glass,
God is within her she will not fall, the circles

of her fingers pressing into the gems of her birthstone.
Her boss was an asshole today. My sister

was a bitch again. My father cares more
about his vodka than he does her.

On the train she thinks everyone sees her
drop her bag. She loses her breath in a panic

to pick it up again. One of her God books fell out—
did they see? Are they out to get her—gang-stalking

their prey like a murder of crows. A murder
so thick you might think it was an omen,

or maybe you might even believe in miracles.
But it's just a gathering like any other—

a flock, a congregation, my mother
filing into a church pew with the Body of Christ.

When I was born my mother says she closed her eyes
and saw Jesus carefully handing me over

like a baby bird—a throat box
with only one remarkable sound.

A new storm of worry landing in her hands.

Wishbone

A bone withers
on the windowsill.

Boiling carcass hurls
its liquid into the pot lid.

Two sisters with feathered
feet streak past the whiff

of marrow. Tomorrow
there will be brown-bagged

turkey sandwiches. Plaid skirts
and saddle shoes, indistinct

and faithless in the closet.
Two bowls of oatmeal, a cup

of tea, a hurried glass of milk.
Nothing else has ever mattered—

that bus is going to come,
and all hope is hitched

to the wishbone.
In a single clack, good luck

lives on the larger side
for the one who can pull it off.

Mother Mary

I hang the rosary on an old shutter hook
outside my window and pray

for the weather to change.
Mary, make it rain on Friday.

Sister Kathleen makes popcorn inside
the classroom on rainy Fridays.

At recess, I'm in the crawlspace behind
your statue, and I let the bugs crawl

up my legs to see how far they'll go
before I am discovered. Mary,

your pink lips are faded from flaying
in the sun too long. I sweat through

my uniform, and stuff tissues into my armpits,
my arms pressed flat against my body to keep them there.

Mary, make it snow so hard
that they'll cancel school altogether.

Don't make me go back inside.
If only I could bend my head into the river and feel

the smoke run out my eyes and ears.
Mary, I want a hurricane, I want wind

so strong my hair unbraids itself.
The other day I grabbed Jimmy Anderson

by his hair and flattened him to the ground
just because I wanted to see something

knocked down. I dragged the needle
of a pin along the inside of my arm

because I liked the way it burned,
like something terrible was finally leeching out.

Every night, I allow this scapula
to cover my heart. My mother says

if I die wearing it I'll go straight to God.
Open your eyes, Mary. Break the sky, Mary.

Child and Flower Cento

No flower like that flower,
which knew itself in the garden.
Lady of silences. Speech
without word. Spur of leaves
and shaking wind. She came
onto the stage in yards
of pearls—flashed her golden
smile and sang.

Your eyes are just like bees,
from the worst pain in the body.
Holding onto the hard earth
so as not to get thrown off.
I don't blame you. You aren't old
enough to know better. Touch
leaf to leaf. Blow the dust
out of your hand. Let it go. Let it go.

Sugar Mountain

You.
You *Oh, to live.*

Your guitar of birds.

You well. You singing.
Your tells. You drinking.

You can't be twenty. You lost
boy. Your fake joy.
Your mother and your dad.
Your life gone bad.

Your gentle kindness.
Your smile. You walk
your daughter down the aisle.

You full of occasion. You easy
to forgive. Your simple fun.
You come undone.

Your flawed
love. Your balloons. *You leaving
there too soon.* Your vodka.
Your magic. Your monster.

You tragic. You dark. You
darker. You drunk. You barker.
Your noisy fair

mind. Your life
number nine.

You godless. You God.
Your buried dead dogs.

You island. Your shame.
You peeling window frame.

Your lonely sleep. Your chair.
Your empty sober stare. *You say
you're leaving home.*

You want to be alone.
Your fresh bottle. Your war.
Your just one more.
Your ragdoll head

pressed to the floor. Your gray
shrinking. Your *what was I
thinking.* You broken-down
barn. You open sky.

You say *just let me die.*

*Ain't it funny
how you feel
when you're finding out its real?*

Your hospital bed.
You back from the dead.

You burden.
Your burden. You carry

along. Your infinite song.

Elegy of Signs
—for my grandfather

The last time I visited your grave I was stuck
in traffic, desperate to move.

I never cared much for graveyards—
all of those expensive rocks, the heavy quiet,

flags and flowers you will never see.
And the thought of your body continuing to decay

right there, right beneath my shoes—
isn't that what rotting is anyway?

Just another kind of slow dying?

I got off the first exit, and found myself crossing
the train tracks that mark the entrance into the cemetery.

You'd like that, I think—the irrelevant part of this story—

how a few drops of early April rain
sprinkled my windshield and I could hear the rumble

of a commuter train approaching.
Does it bother you—the way they zip by like that—

that perpetual state of hurry? Or is it the endless
freight train, dragging its worn-out thunder of metal.

Does it make you brood in the box? Make you
want cancer all over again?

It's been decades since I bent over your body
and wept—pressed my lips to your sunken cheek,

astonished at how fast the body goes cold—
how quickly we can become entirely emptied of love

and esprit. I laid my head upon your chest
and recited three Hail Mary's aloud. I was thirteen,

and I believed she could hear them.

And maybe it was because in the end I swear
you looked as if you saw something in the room.

Your skinny arms reaching out, almost in panic,
pointing to the corner of the ceiling.

You tried to show us, tried to say what it was,

but no one in the room, not Gramma, not your children,
none of us could hear past the sickness gurgling in your throat.

We kissed your head, said things would be ok,
and you laid back again, annoyed.

In the graveyard, I tried to find evidence of you
anywhere—a tap on my shoulder, a playful tug

on my sleeve, or perhaps I would lose my breath
in the feeling of a sudden, sentient wind.

A cloud of gnats arrived, dancing
out from along the river, as if newly

born from mud and melting snow.

They came upon me like a net, flew in my face
and my eyes. I spit one out of my mouth and left.

Sometimes I think I've outgrown your memory.
Each day, I think of you a little less, forget

the details of one of your stories, put another picture
away and you become a little more gone.

And I hardly think about those final hours,
the way my cells burned and split

over the thought of losing you. And the way you panted
and genuflected repeatedly, preparing yourself, pointing

to the corner as if you could actually see something
coming for you. Your sick eyes, all the small tunnels

of your body freezing and seizing at the sight of it.

One for Sorrow

Fill me empty, fill me

goodbye. Fill me silent song

circle—locked doors and cold

kitchen floors. Fill me drop-

box of the wilted unwanted.

The quiet scars of all sealed

things. Fill throat pouch

solace, infinite. My terrible mind—

sky in the river and no wings.

IV

Glimpse

With fearless urgency, the bird

crashed into my bedroom window.

Wings flying toward wings and then breaking

on what must have seemed like another bird

in some peculiar piece of sky.

It landed half-dead on my front porch

like an offering. Little bag of air,

inflating and deflating—twitching into

or out of every ache. I watched and waited

until it stopped. Rolled the body with a plastic

shovel into my kid's blue sand bucket.

Carried it to the edge of the yard,

and then tossed it into the woods.

And nothing moved, or flinched, or changed.

Sun boring into every window of the house.

Four for a Boy

His heart   is strong—   the storm

that gives push   to rivers.   It gallops

through the monitor   like a collision

of clouds.   How is it, then,   my sister

knew: do not setup   the nursery,

become   a different   kind of prepared—

a virus will ruin his brain—make the heart

for nothing—for all its reaches,   it is just

a sound,   a flick of a coiled doorstop

that will wobble   to a still.

And when they empty her, she will swell again

to bursting—   for the breath not taken,

and all the rains he left behind.

Two for Joy

Joy Geraldine, Joy Geraldine,
making your shape in the fifteenth
week. Joy, the quickening
in my sister's belly
where another did not become.
Can you feel him, Joy?
When you stretch the walls
that only siblings can touch—
do you kick against his footprint?
Your older brother
who left without breath—
without even a death rattle.

You are not the bird, Joy
Geraldine—not the song, or the flower.
You are switchgrass in an open field
and the childish urge to run through it.
Tell me something good,
Joy Geraldine. Say Joy is careless
light in the dust wiped
off the dresser. Joy—the breeze
that fills the gap between crib frame
and wall. We are ready to fall
in your wind, Joy,
should you decide to arrive at all.

Dominoes

Are you ready, Mom?

he asks, kneeling beside
our twisted ladder

of assembled dominoes.

We both know each bright
rectangle carries

a risk of undoing.

Outside the world
is going on unrehearsed—

days colliding like pearls

of moisture rolling
down a blade of grass.

I became a mom
only once, you know.

You are the bike I learned

to ride. An imperishable
knowing lock-boxed

heavy into my brain.

Your sloughed-off
cells pinned to my bones

the way I remain

hooked to my mother,
even now. This pattern

we made—the motion

will reside within it
only briefly, like ripples

across a lake—the way you

arrived, only once—
a wave moving through,

but not with, the water.

Six for Gold

When my six-year-old asks me where
he came from—how he, you know,
got inside my belly, he is swinging a broken
tree branch around in the backyard.
Just swinging to feel the air molecules,
to hear the faint whistle of resistance.
The invisible turbulence satisfies something
for both of us—disturbing what you can't see.
You were a star I took for my own, I say.
But how does it work, he asks, you know,
getting the star into your belly? I rub
my hands together vigorously and then slowly
pull them apart like a wizard commanding
an invisible orb. I tell him to try—
keep rubbing your hands as fast as you can,
and when you are ready, stop—wait
for the energy to arrive between your palms.
He doesn't know this is just a game, just
our nerves responding to friction. He gently
packs his hands around what he feels, a warm
snowball. I say imagine that energy gathering
into your belly. When you arrived, an old star
collapsed and exploded, and in a huge
blast you landed inside me. He tosses his secret
ball into the sky—it's gone somewhere
we will never find. Like gold crashing into a rock,
or sinking into the bottom of a river, I say.
I can tell he is no longer listening—his eyes
are back to the branch. I smile and scoop
him up before he can grab it again, tickling
his side to make him giggle. He wiggles
in my arms, laughter bright and bursting,
this boy who came to me like gold.

After Winter

It would not stop raining—
water passing through water,
testing the rivers and pressing
the dams. Water weathering
with determined divination—it bled
through the wood beams and taunted
our foreheads as we slept.
I put the kids in the car for a drive
because it felt good to think the water
was something we could skim
along, like water bugs. I splashed
through every puddle to hear
their ferocious squeals. *Look Mom,*
there is heaven, my son said, as we drove
passed the cemetery. Water bathing sun-
bleached stones, washing over dead
names, and filling green plastic
pots of long-gone flowers.
Look ahead, I said. I think I see a thin
glimmer reaching behind clouds.
It just happens, I tell them—the natural
pull of sun and moon. The world
is destroyed in one part and renewed
in the other. Each tick a death
and a blossom, proportionately reckless.
My muscles twitch-itching the whole way
like water rippling under the skin.

Depression Cento

There is no other way to say this:
I am in the thrall of bony whiteness—

how several madnesses are born—
a season dry in the fireplace—this strange

church I am building, excited
by wind, the sudden feel of life—to be

redeemed from fire by fire. No—
let me start again. I can say it now:

In nature there are few sharp lines. The open
window is full of a voice. The sound

of bones touched together. Among
those lost trees—dew on the sleeve of hours.

Anatomy of a Home

On every wall, knotted pine
bares lifelines.

Checks and splits flaw the wood
beams where fibers compress

into empty space. A daughter bites
her graham cracker into the shape

of a moon and laughs. A son fusses
over a puzzle on the floor—piece

by piece, bucks interlocking
on an unknown hill. They are waiting

for the first flakes of another storm,
the baby to wake from her nap.

Outside, bald flashes of wood
ache where ice fractured branches.

Cells harden beneath the crack
of bark, the way silica remains

liquid as it is super-cooled into glass.
A father is away at work—wind pulls

and stretches the tree roots.
A mother, the heartwood, alive

inside death, log on log into fire.

At the Market

I have to tell you—bright light

organic. Clear water polish.

I have to tell you shine. Perfect

patterns of leaping color. Metal

carts pushed by sleepwalking

mothers and lost single men. Polite,

the boxes and bottles stand.

The lemons and apples lie down.

But all of this will perish.

In the middle of my life, I know

the rat that sinks its tooth

into the pulp. I have seen the claw

pull on a scrap wish, unsayable.

I have to tell you the sound of want—

twisted and stretched in those so many

mouths, the orchestra of orchids behind me.

Grease

The world was not my undoing.
It was something smaller.

A house inside of a house.

A place where darker veins eel together.

And my body
on a mattress looking up.   Not at the world.

But at minutes turning loose off the clock.
You need rest, my husband says. *The children are
playing in the yard.*

When did the sound of joy
become an urgency? I wondered.

You need to relax.

And would you believe me
if I told you that in this place there was a door

deeper. A little capsule falling
down my throat like an anchor.   A synthetic
heaviness, and then sleep.

It is that room.

Still as a bar of iron.

No wind or children or touch of hands on hands.
Not even that voice crawling its way in:

Soon, you will have to make dinner.
Put the baby on your hip—mighty mother able.

What was I then but skin
splayed over a match.

Froth on a simmer.   My life

rushing out like grease spitting out of a pan.

Tapering off of Clonazepam

I only want to return
to where the water isn't gentle.

Can you get back what you lost?

What I lost lives within a place I can't unknow.

There are many knots to unsnarl.
The numbness will want to show its teeth.

But the old dress still fits. I only eat a flake
of white now—smaller than a grain of sand.
My blood sparkles alive and on fire.

Do you remember the storm?

I remember the microburst. The sound
of laughing metal in sky. Like Truth
arriving—rain and wind barreling down the street
in a straight line. And the collective snap
of all it took with it. But we were spared.

What about the birds?

Imagine a story impossible to tell. A story born
from birds. When wind and water flex their muscle

wings know what to do. All we could do was watch.

Was it a kind of relief?

I never said I wasn't thankful.
There were small victories. Clay sealed
into the cracks. The kids singing in the back of the car.
But pills made thin my thinking.

Can you still feel it in the half-dose?

I feel half-bloomed. A dangle of roots
down concrete stairs. A page still blank
and not quite ready.

Stay here. There is time
for one more baby. Ice yet to thaw
before the peas go in the ground.

Let's go over this again. I do not know the path
my body made through this house. I'm afraid
I might have taken my husband's capacity for love.
I fear the kids are birds with no trees.

What do you feel now?

I feel like the pulse that lives in an afterthought. The last
light that masses itself into flame before nightfall.

It is a kind of dance—the way a body shudders
to rhythm and breath, and how we put our fingers
there to feel it.

To be bent back by wind and water only
to straighten out again.

I want to shelter my family
from the storm, I can no longer be the storm.

Godless

It is not The Word
that brings me to a perfect halt.

It is a hard, unbreakable consonant
that hurts my mouth like an olive pit.

Something clean, something
finished in my inner ear.

And outside:
All lung and no breath. It is easy

to remember this kind of stillness.
I want it on my skin

like a tick. I want to lie down
like a dog for what it might give me.

In the compost across the yard,
bugs suck at my scraps.

Fire soot—coffee grind—
apple core—and I think:

Save nothing. And I am in love.
I am in love with this quiet church.

Reincarnate

I open the backdoor and baptize
myself in a clean rush of garden air.

The crows announce themselves—
a sub-song of quick,

downward cuts from tall pines.
A child buries her head

into the warmth of my waist. I look
down and my own face

is looking back, like the dull glow
of moon in earthlight.

I am amazed by my own body—
the assembly of cells building and rebuilding

without incident, or song, or ceremony.
I comb skeins of hair, brush clipped

fingernails into a dustpan—slivers
of life I simply collect and throw

away. I sink my knife deep into the flesh
of vegetables—eat the light hidden

in the tomato. The slow horse of my heart
clopping as if it has nothing better to do.

Raven

Echo into the turning
wind

Then stillness
sinking into the lamp-light

tell me
parting bird

black eyes have all the dreaming

Selva Oscura

I.   Purgatorio

Should you decide that I might be saved, consider the ink
of my wicked pride—my white overexposed nakedness.

I am an unplaceable woman. A tired bitch
announced in heavy footfalls down the stairs.

The bird of my lover's heart sags on the vine like fruit
over-fattening between two worlds.

The cuckoo clock teases out time. With every door slap
my old dog throws a sigh from his dirty floor bed.

I want my dog to die. His rancid fur stains oil in the hardwood,
his knowing eyes beg me to let him perish.

I thought I understood love, but it is just a feral
need of the body, a tedious, aging thirst.

Chemicals flush through mazes—a regular sickness
reaching out, but my pen needs to make a name of it.

If Hell is fire, then may heaven be a cool wet wind
at the car window for my dog's final drive.

In the middle of this dark wood, let leaves drop
into dumb air. Let me glitter between the two halves.

II.   Paradiso

The ash of my dog is not what I expected.
There are shards of bone—fragments in the fragment of his weight,

I let myself say the world has no meaning.
The words leak effortlessly, like blood rushing from a wound.

I thought myself more a woman than *lie down*
lie down. The man has needs, the man has chemicals too.

The children are each their own empyrean. It is enough to have
them, fleeting as it may be, like an unkindness of ravens, and then none.

My dead dog was handed back like a bag of flour. I placed him into
a small box on the shelf. I lie to the children and say *he's still here*.

Maybe we are no more than our human peaks. The heaven of us lives
in the swells and stretches before the inevitable crack.

I stroke the cedar box of my dog's dust. Good
old boy. My purest friend. I do not feel you at all.

A child's hand fits into a mother's like two gears clinked together.
Two gears clink together and that is the still-point-poem before the turn.

NOTES

"Depression Cento" sources lines from AR Ammons, Carolyn Forché, Jorie Graham, Linda Gregg, Robert Hass, Yusef Komunyakaa, Ann Lauterbach, H. Leivick, Mina Loy, Muriel Rukeyser.

"Child and Flower Cento" sources lines from Randall Jarrell, Jorie Graham, Robert Hayden, May Swenson, Conrad Aiken, T. S. Eliot, Mikhail Naimy, Allen Ginsberg, Donald Hall.

"Joan" italicized lines are from John 2:17 of the Bible.

"We Who Are Nothingness" draws its title and the following lines from John Frederick Nim's poem, "Prayer:" "Love cannot fill us" and "No dream-caress nor actual."

"Raven" is an erasure of Edgar Allen Poe's "The Raven."

"Four for A Boy" and "Two for Joy" are for my sister Emma, my nephew Shane, and my niece Joy.

"Sugar Mountain" italicized lines are from Neil Young's song of the same name.

Inspiration and knowledge of crows that inspired many of these poems, especially "Nesting," came from *Bird Brains* by Candace Savage.

ACKNOWLEDGMENTS

Grateful acknowledgement is made to the editors of the following journals and anthologies where these poems, sometimes in earlier versions, first appeared:

Atticus Review: "Elegy of Signs"

Birmingham Poetry Review: "Depression Cento" and "A Proposal"

Brittany Noakes Poetry Award Finalist: "Grease"

Chiron Review: "Elena Says"

Construction Magazine: "Six for Gold"

Frontier Poetry: Industry Prize 2019 semi-finalist: "Elena Says"

Inklett Magazine: "The Birds"

Mass Poetry, Poem of The Moment: "Godless"

Mom Egg Review: "Cockcrow"

Moon City Review: "Knead"

Nelle: "Four for a Boy"

Open: Journal of Arts & Letters: "911," "Glimpse," "Grease," "Now I Lay Them Down to Sleep," "Reincarnate," "The Sentinel," "Vessel"

Salamander: "Elegy of Color"

Shake The Tree: "Nesting" (formally titled, "A Mother's Nature"), "One For Sorrow," "Swaddle"

The Sunday Poet: "The First Gunshot"

Tupelo Quarterly: Poetry Prize semi-finalist: "Crow Funeral"

Yes, Poetry: "Never to Be Told"

"Elegy of Color" is reprinted in the 12th edition, *Compact Bedford Introduction to Literature* by Michael Meyer and D. Quentin Miller, 2020.

Early drafts of several poems were written during *Tupelo Quarterly*'s 30/30 poetry project.

This work was made possible by the support of The Vermont Studio Center and a fellowship from The Sustainable Arts Foundation.

Immense gratitude to Denton Loving and the entire EastOver Press team for believing in my work and helping to usher it into the world.

Thank you to my family and the following friends and writers who provided their support and comments regarding the poems in this collection without whom this book would not be possible: Michael Kleber-Diggs, Michael Schmeltzer, Heather Bell, Clint Margrave, Kristin Hersh, Sarah Sousa, Sarah Anderson, Liz Marlow, and so many more.

Special thanks to my poetry brother, Matt Miller, for always believing in me and my work and for graciously editing this collection.

Thank you, Dick Foster, for the incredible portrait of me that became the cover image of this book.

Thank you to my children, Henry, Coralie, and Maeve, for the immeasurable joy you bring to my life. I do not take a single day for granted.

Finally, a huge thank you to Bert Foster for being my best friend and biggest supporter. Thank you for taking care of me all these years and always being there even in the hardest times. I love you more and more every day.

CPSIA information can be obtained
at www.ICGtesting.com
Printed in the USA
FSHW021208110222
88230FS